THE POISONING OF THE FOUNDER

ACHARYA OF

HARE KRSNA

MOVEMENT

by

Nanda Gopala

Gotham Books

30 N Gould St.
Ste. 20820, Sheridan, WY 82801
https://gothambooksinc.com/

Phone: 1 (307) 464-7800

© 2023 *Nanda Gopala*. All rights reserved.

No part of this book may be reproduced, stored in a retrieval system, or transmitted by any means without the written permission of the author.

Published by Gotham Books (November 21, 2023)

ISBN: 979-8-88775-399-7 (H)
ISBN: 979-8-88775-397-3 (P)
ISBN: 979-8-88775-398-0 (E)

Because of the dynamic nature of the Internet, any web addresses or links contained in this book may have changed since publication and may no longer be valid.

The views expressed in this work are solely those of the author and do not necessarily reflect the views of the publisher, and the publisher hereby disclaims any responsibility for them.

PART 1

There are two reasons why the founder of the Hare Krsna movement was poisoned. The first one is personal aggrandizement, meaning Bhavananda wanted to become world leader. The second reason, which is a little bit more deeper and hideous, is the fact that the Free Masons or the Jesuits, the Cabal, the Illuminati want a one world religion and they have used Bhavananda to infiltrate the movement along with various other men and take it over by killing the founder.

So, these two aspects, we're going to look at in detail. The first aspect is the fact that Bhavananda, when he came to Australia as the world leader, was hideously gay. He was a homosexual. He was prancing around to all the gay nightclubs in Sydney, in King's Cross, the temple that we had to buy for him, sometimes being carried out of the gay bars, too drunk to walk. This is the world leader of the Hare Krsna movement, the world guru. This is what he claims himself in his news interviews in various videos on YouTube.

Bhavananda Swami ISKCON is on YouTube and you can see for yourself how this man is. He's an overt malignant narcissist, grandiose, very dangerous and they have no care for anyone. The fact that the world leadership position was put in his grasp is enough to show you that he actually did poison Prabhupad. That in itself is enough to show you that by becoming world leader, he poisoned Prabhupad. The poisoning of Prabhupad is without doubt now, it's being proven in very high scientific circles. Cadmium was 250 times the normal amount, and a lot of money has been spent on that research. So, fortunately, that's all under the bridge now, that's all being done. That's the proof that this entire case is resting on that Nityananda the Truth committee compiled and he has actually made a $50,000 reward, which I've offered back to him because of the work that he has already done. But there's a $50,000 reward on whoever poisoned Prabhupad, meaning they know someone poisoned him.

The exclusive position I'm in is that I was Bhavananda's first disciple in Australia. I received both Gayatri and Japa initiation, so I was watching him. I joined five years before he came on and I received Prabhupad's blessings, but I was forced to collect for him for 40 years on the street. So those particular contracts that I have with Bhavananda are unique, and that's the reason why I'm being called upon to address this.

Now, it looks like no one else in the world can do this, because there are only little snippets of information here and there, but because I took it on twelve years ago in absolute solitude and absolutely determined to get to the answer, all the right information has been coming into me. So, for twelve years in total isolation, I've been putting this together, and have come to a very hearty conclusion, which is actually summarized by his actions in Australia, which a lot of you didn't get to see. We now see him on the Vyasasann in Vrindavan, India. Now, because I recently got a lawyer to take it on here in Australia, he escaped back to India where he can't be touched by us in Australia. That's the reason why he's just now in India. But he does have Australian citizenship and he's just claimed all the Australian properties as the sole heir. Really that speaks for itself. His number one prime goal the entire time is simply to inherit all of the ISKCON properties. And that's why he made ISKCON incorporated of

West Bengal and claimed all the properties. And that's why he's maintained his relationship with Alfred Ford, Henry Ford's great grandson, the 33-degree free mason.

So those two aspects, when you put them together, you'll see that there are certainly two motives for the poisoning of Prabhupad. One is to take complete control of the movement, which is what he did. And the second one is simply as a puppet for the Cabal, for whatever reason. But because we know the Cabal run the police, the courts, the medicine, everything, it's not without question that this isn't an aspect to it. But this isn't the aspect that I'm harboring on. I'm harboring on the aspect of his actions in Sydney that nobody got to see, which clearly proved he poisoned the founder to become the world leader, which he was not in any way qualified to do. The truth is, Prabhupad had named two successors, Gour Govinda and Radha Govinda Swami, and had asked his secretary Tamala to express that to the devotees.

For five days, Tamala returned to Prabhupad and Prabhupad asked him, "Have you told them yet?" And he kept replying, "No." And on the 6th day, when he again returned, he said, "No, I still haven't told him." Prabhupad then said, "Now, it is all finished!" And Prabhupad himself knew he was being poisoned that's why he asked his sister Pisima to cook for him, but Bhavananda got rid of Pisima, as they did the doctors who were sent to aid Prabhupad, who also said that he was being poisoned. They swiftly got rid of these doctors.

One young boy saw Bhavananda sprinkling dust on Prabhupad's food, and he asked him, "What is that?" and Bhavananda said, "Oh, it's magic dust." Bhavananda himself said so in a video that he was the only one who had access to Prabhupad. He was a body man. Nothing went in or out without him. And Bakticuru was a chemist who knew all about Cadmium. They were the only three who were allowed to be near Prabhupad. So this is a very, very distasteful subject. Nobody wants to hear this and everybody wants to avoid it.

I had just outlined the facts and you can decide for yourself. However, my avenue is that I'm the prime witness in Australia, which is where he came. He claimed the whole of Australia. And he's now the heir to all the Australian properties, no doubt the Indian property. In fact, he created ISKCON incorporated and the BBTI. The first thing Bhavananda did was change the entire structure of ISCON from books to candles. This is the most illegal and offensive thing that could possibly be done as Prabhupad said that books were the maintenance of the movement.

The reason we all joined Prabhupad's movement was because of the books. We joined up to distribute his books; that's what we did everyday. We did nothing else. We had no other interest. We were distributing Prabhupad's books and we felt fantastic. We knew how much benefit we were giving to people.

Bhavananda made that illegal in Australia. He banned anyone who wanted to do it. Gopinath died as a result of being banned for wanting to sell books and not candles. He got banned and he died as a result of that banning.

There's another boy in Melbourne that Bhavananda molested. That boy was so disgusted that he burned Bhavananda's house down. So Bhavananda jailed him and the headmaster who complained. And when that boy got out of jail, he hung himself. The boy's name is Matsya. The headmaster's name is Achyuta Edward Brungardt. Edward was banished to New Zealand for even bringing this up. The point is, the poor boy hung himself because he was molested by Bhavananda, and whether he hung himself or it was a case of murder is yet to be seen.

It turns out Bhavananda has molested thousands of boys in India. Even when he was the temple president in New York, he was making the boys stand out on the balcony all night long in the freezing cold New York, which we know is a part of satanic child ritual abuse. They traumatize children, get their blood, and drink it. It's called adrenochrome. I don't need to go into the details about that, but we know that Bhavananda came from Hollywood; his best friend was Andy Warhol who was known for his feasts on fetuses.

It looks like Bhavananda was very well involved in the adrenochrome and Hollywood elites. That's why he was incredibly good looking. It's why he became the world leader of ISKCON, simply because of his looks. In fact, in one video, he said himself, "Prabhupad said that I was the most handsome man in ISKCON." Prabhupad was talking about beauty in a woman. Bhavananda said, "So what are the traits of beauty in a man?" -- He's really twisted. Prabhupad says, "Just like you, you are the most handsome man in ISKCON."

This movement is meant to save the world, but it's being led by a criminal organization at the moment who have jeopardized our books and all of our temples and are forcing all the people who join to become slaves. That happened to me for 45 years, I was a slave on the street in a wig, lying to people 24 hours a day, seven days a week. I had to lie. No, I'm not Sridhar Hare Krsna devotee, I'm just selling candles. I'm a university student and I make these candles. So, the trauma that you get from having to lie to people, it's indescribable. You have no idea. Anyone who hasn't been through this has got no idea what a narcissist is and what they can put you through. Bhavananda is the king of narcissists. Because he was the head of ISKCON and the head of Mayapur and claims to be Prabhupad's best servant which he himself says in a video. It turns out he was killing people left, right and center.

I can prove that he ordered Sulochana, Aindra, and Kadamba Kanana's assassination and that he sent dacoits to kill Sridhar Maharaj who was Prabhupad's God brother and who was given the TOPV to manage. Those dacoits came back with the bomb that he had sent to kill Sridhar, and that blew off Bhakti Raghava's leg. And Bhavananda shot those two dacoits point blank with a shotgun. He was the only one in ISKCON with a gun.

Recently, a 400 million dollar court case was won and the truth is, the lawyer, when he actually heard the details of the case, he offered $400 million and hoped that they would get away with that. However, it's a lot more severe. It's not just about the molesting of children; it was on the borders of satanic child ritual abuse. There was a number of children being tortured and raped, and were not just friendly dealings. It was satanic child ritual abuse on a massive scale that $400 million was paid out to. Some of them have committed suicide, and a lot of them are not here anymore. A lot of men in Australia have committed suicide. All of Bhavananda's closest men have all hung themselves. And this court case is just an example of the extent of the abuse that was going on. This is not just an ordinary schoolroom abuse, this is bordering on satanic child ritual abuse. It must be.

Various boys in India have said that Bhavananda would beat them with the stick they used for beating a gong in the temple, a huge stick, really hard on their head. They all had bruises, and they were made to go up into his room and he would beat them very hard just to traumatize them. It's called grooming. You're getting them ready for something big. A lot of parents are happy that their kids are in school and that's the last they see of them. In fact, many orphans were picked up from railway stations and whether they get trafficked, who knows? That's why Kadamba Kanana was shot in the back. He was sent in specifically to clean up the Vindarban Gurukula, and he was shot in the back and said it himself that it was an inside job.

At this stage, ISKCON has fallen into a whirlpool that's irretrievable. But the point is because Bhavananda was the head of the New York Temple and then he became leader of Mayapur which is world Headquarters, pretty much, he has been running the show even while Prabhupad was here, but particularly after Prabhupad left, he was totally in charge. There was no one higher than him. He was the one. And then there were ten gurus. Apparently, they've been elected under him, but they were just actually wimps compared to him. Everyone knew he was in charge. That was the impression he was giving on the altars in Mayapur. I was there at that time when they had just made the eleven. So, the basic thing is that the whole thing was a lie, that those eleven men that were enlisted, they all lied. Everything on top of that was a lie.

Now that Bhavananda is running our temple at the Vedic planetarium, once a lie is made, you cannot not just build on it. So, the first thing about Bhavanada is that he was wearing saffron. But firstly, he made Sulochana perform oral sex on him in New Vrndavan. And he continued wearing saffron. He was also caught having sex in a taxi with a taxi driver and he asked Prabhupad to let him remain in saffron because it's a good look. Barbaranda was just into the looks. It was essential he remained in saffron. But the saffron robe means that you're an absolute celibate. But he was lying. And the only proof that we have at this stage that Bhavananda didn't poison Prabhupad is he himself saying "No, I didn't. It's a preposterous idea." But he is the only one who's saying "No, I didn't poison Prabhupad." However, it's been proven countless times in Australia that he is a liar. The whole time he was wearing saffron, he was entirely lying. He was constantly having homosexual relationships in India with young boys and taxi drivers or whoever he could. And that went on and on and that's all been documented in Australia, too.

But lying is one thing, and for a Hare Krsna - we're trained as Brahmans as a priest, when you join the Harrison movement, you become a Brahmana. And the first quality of Brahmana is truthfulness. If you don't have that basis of truthfulness, you're not qualified as a Brahmana. But this is the leader. This is the world leader. This is not just a Bhakta. This is the man who became the world leader and is in all of our television interviews, the early interviews. He is the world leader of the Hare Krishna movement and the number one guru. So that in itself is a lie. And that's proves he's lying when he says he didn't poison Prabhupad. And that at the moment is the only thing that's upholding the fact that he didn't poison Prabhupad. That he says, "I didn't." But he's a liar.

So really, I've given the outlines, the details, I really don't need to go on. And we can keep this book very short. The main one is about Sridhar Maharaj being killed; Dacoits, being sent, and that a couple of his initiating gurus told me in confidence that he'd sent dacoits to kill him.

He'd paid dacoits to kill Sridhar, plus the taxi where Tamal was killed in, that was messed around with, the oil cap, etcetera, were played with so that the car would explode and the taxi driver just ran and he got paid a huge amount.

And of course, the other thing is, Jayapataka has a couple of children. He's the other world leader. He's got children that he's paying the mother hush money in South Africa. So these aspects, you just look at the top of the movement and perhaps we can clean the movement up. If enough people get to hear this, they'll know what's happening in the movement and everyone's just terrified because of Ford - Ambarish who, at this stage, hasn't really committed any major offenses, apart from the fact that he's a freemason. But he's kept a pretty slick profile because of his position as great grandson of Henry Ford. But Bhavananda has been a bit more promiscuous because he thought he had the run of the reigns and no one picked him out. But I certainly did. No one else has it like I do, that's for sure. I challenge anyone to come up with details like this and I'm going to leave it like that, just with these details. They're fine and they're meticulous, but they're certainly true and they're all there.

PART 2

So, I'll lightly touch on the Course in Miracles from Jesus before in this book and the fact that it was printed from a slaughterhouse I opened a temple in which is the darkest place on earth - Jesus uses those exact terms. I need to emphasize the fact where the Course in Miracles and Krishna consciousness run side by side. And that's in the sentence Jesus uses in the course. He said, "You couldn't wait to get your heart cleansed so that God's mirror can shine on it." That's exactly the same as the philosophy of Krishna consciousness; that you're meant to cleanse the heart by chanting the Hare Krishna mantra. That sound vibration enters through the substratum of sound, it enters the heart and it cleanses the heart where Krishna is eternally residing at Paramatma.

Jesus uses the term "Holy Spirit" and Prabhupad uses the term "Paramatma", but it's Krishna residing within the heart. That's where the Course in Miracles and Prabhupad's teaching runs side in line. And why this book might be quite beneficial for anyone who might then go on to look at the Course in Miracles and onto Prabhupad's books.

There are a few aspects about Bhavananda in Sydney. One was that he made us sell this thing. It was about a foot long and it had two balls at the end of it. And it was carved out of wood and it looked exactly like a male genital. He made the women go out on the street and rub men up and down with it, saying it was a massager. They then turned it into a moose with four wheels. This was the paraphernalia of the ISKCON movement. They would get men on the street and rub them with it, and then they were selling stickers. So, Lord Jaganath is the deity in Jaganath Puri. He's a deity of Krishna with two big eyes. What they did was they wrote "smile" over that deity of Lord Jaganath, and would sell it as a sticker to put onto people's back bumper bars above the exhaust. It was very offensive that they wrote it over the Lord Jaganath who is the most famous deity in Jaganath Puri.

These are the sort of blasphemies that were happening under Bhavananda. The whole thing is so hideous, this entire story, that it certainly should be produced in a movie. But why it's going to be difficult to make a movie out of it is because you'll never get an actor like Prabhupad. You'll never be able to get someone like Prabhupad. The best thing is to be able to get the videos that are available now on YouTube. And certainly, a movie can be produced; but probably, these details are more important at this stage. And it's very enticing to know that at this early stage of the book, a movie has been proposed for it.

In Sydney, as I said, we had to do three months of long marathons, but the secretary Chittahari lost the entire amount that we collected, staying out all night, on a heroin deal for two years in a row. Bhavananda had two very close men that was Chittahari and Naresvara. Naresvara was in charge of the BBT and Chittahari was the national secretary.

Naresvara went on Facebook recently and said, "I know I'm a criminal but I have masses of money to pay the corrupt system. Catch me if you can." They destroyed our Spiritual Sky which was an incense making factory that ISKCON was based on. Spiritual Sky was another form of bonafide revenue. It was the only form of bonafide income that Prabhupad allowed, making incense. Spiritual Sky had a Hare Krishna mantra on the package, incense oil, soaps and shampoos. It was a very nice and successful company because it had a picture of Krishna on the front and it was totally transcendental. A beautiful company. The whole company was transcendental, you could tell. But Naresvara destroyed that company, threw Jai Dharma out in the street and I was sent on the bus party. I was the pujari of the deities that we had on our Cola River farm. A beautiful farm with cows. We were growing our own food. But soon as Bhavananda came in, he destroyed that farm, they sold it. They took the deities to the King's Cross temple where we had to build a whole upstairs for Bhavananda, where he had his harem of all homosexuals. And then they took the Deities to a funeral parlor in North Sydney. From a beautiful farm setting, it became the busiest, most disgusting area in King's Cross simply because it was a homosexual hangout.

And from there, they went to a place, a funeral parlor in North Sydney, which was also on the biggest and the busiest intersection in Australia. These were the deities that Prabhupad himself brought from India. Very beautiful deities. Prabhupad said, "I'm leaving you, (meaning the Lord). I'm leaving you with these mlecchas. I hope they can look after you." So at the moment, they're on the busiest intersection in Australia. All the traffic was going into the harbor bridge and they're not happy. Of course, Bhavananda put them there. But not only did he put them there, he was living with a man who had had a transgender operation and was wearing a sari to worship those deities. He was living in the same flat with that man.

That's the standard of degradation that Bhavananda introduced. He was prancing round in gay bars in front of all of his disciples and boys and girls who'd given their lives to the movement who had to collect for him day in, day out. He had no worries at all prancing around in front of them in a big crimson cloak with a T-shirt saying "I am a guru" and bringing boyfriends home from the gay bars and being carried out of the gay bars too drunk to even walk. He had no problem at all in demonstrating himself like that. He could not care at all. And that's what shows me that he had no care at all to poison Prabhupad the way he treated his disciples. All he did was say "Oh, I had sex with a man. Now go away all you, disciples. I'm no longer your guru, but give me all the money." He kept all the establishments and he's now the sole heir to all Australian properties. But the fact that he treated his disciples like that "No, I simply had sex and I can do what I like." It's on the video. All he had to do was wear white instead of saffron. But you can tell that he's covering up this hideous thought that he poisoned Prabhupad with all these distractions being thrown around. The main thing is the way that he treated his disciples with no care at all, and with no care at all about Krishna consciousness. No longer interested at all, he became a model. Professional model. That's the opposite of Krishna consciousness. Krishna consciousness means we're not these bodies. That's all he was, as a model. Now I'm a body and you can pay me to photograph my body.

Krishna has recently put me through the most unbelievable experience to understand what a narcissist is. I invited a person, was pretending to be a devotee in my farm. I started farming--- it was Varnashram Cow Protection Farm here in Australia, and I made a terrible mistake of inviting someone who I'd briefly met at New Govardhan. He suddenly turned on me and threatened to kill me, took all my cars, my motorbike, my money, my house, all my things I'd been growing. He took absolutely everything he could and dragged me out in the forest to die. I had a broken Achilles heel when I invited him here and he took my walking stick so I couldn't walk. I haven't been able to shop in three years. He took every car. My twin bought me a brand new car. He destroyed that. I never got to use it. He's locked me in. He got money to take me to the doctor. He took me to the doctor and he started screaming at the nurse, so I couldn't get the appointment. Krishna has shown me what narcissists are like through the example of this person.

I was never up close to Bhavananda. I never actually talked to him. The only thing he ever said to was one thing, "Just keep your nose clean." The only words he ever said to me as the guru. So, this narcissist has shown me what narcissists are like. I haven't been able to shop for three years now. Krishna has kept me alive here in the forest. I'm completely alone with this narcissist, threatening to kill me and stealing everything he can from me. All my money and vehicles and communication, everything he can, and just laughing about it makes them happy. That's the way they treat people. Krishna has shown me point blank what a narcissist is like. And Bhavananda is a grandiose narcissist. Until you've been targeted by one, you won't know what they're like. That's why I have to express this story about what narcissists are like. They're just the most evil and selfish people you cannot imagine. And that's simply the way Bhavananda has acted. And that's why this book has got some fruit to it because of the actions I've witnessed Bhavananda do. It's not just whether someone gave Cadmium to Prabhupad or not that this whole thing is resting.

No, it is 20 years of criminal activity that he's responsible for. The poisoning is just a side issue, of course, he poisoned Prabhupad when you hear his entire story; of course, he poisoned Prabhupad when you hear all the glimmerings, all the icing on the cake. Well, if he sent dacoits to kill Sridhar Maharaj and if he killed Aindra for writing the book that I'm just about to publish, which was about the gurus, the same with Sulochana. It was called the guru business! Sulochana was killed brutally just before he was about to release the guru business story. But Sulochana was a special case because he was made to perform oral sex on Bhavananda. And that's why Bhavananda had to kill him. Because if that became known, Bhavananda could no longer be a sanyasi or a guru. So that's why I've included that dreadful photo of Sulochana cut from the waist up and shot in the head. And that brings another whole story about Radanath and the Nasringha Swami who Radanath told that he had ordered the killing of Sulochana. Nasringha Swami mysteriously died also.

So we have two GBCS in Australia. Not just Ramar Swami, but this guy called Devamrita Swami who was the temple president of New Vindarban. And he paid the money to have Sulochana killed. He's now our GBC. And not only that, he ran off with bags of money after it happened, knowing he was guilty. He ran off with as much money as he could. And he winds up in Australia as our GBC.

A boy joined the same day as me. His name was Bala, and he became chosen as Bhavanada's personal servant. And he ended up admitting himself to a psychiatric ward. He obviously was so mentally disturbed by what Bhavananda put him through that he admitted himself to a psychiatric ward. Several of the other men that were with Bhavananda hung themselves. Madamangla das, Bhutanath das, Sarvaksha das Vashupati das, Prit das, Matiya das and another one was found face down. And there's a whole list of others who took Bhavananda as a guru and they hung themselves. So all this just appears as a story up until the point where you realize, that actually Bhavananda is still running the movement. He's still in charge of the temple of Vedic Planetarium and he's still appearing on the Vyasasan in India in Vrindarvan as if nothing ever happened. This is the way a narcissist works. They just cover your knowledge and pretend that what they're saying is the absolute truth. And also, all of them are blackmailing each other.

But the fact is that they are running the movement at the moment, is the importance of this book. Otherwise, there's no meaning to this book. But the fact that they are presently running the movement, changes this book from just a very sad story to a present catastrophe that is much like the Catholic Church. And unless it's brought to attention like the Catholic Church, they will get away with it. At the moment, ISKCON is owned by the Catholic Church.

***

Srila Prabhupada Memories, Part 3 by HG Malati Devi Dasi

ISKCON Columbus · 250 views · Streamed 1 year ago

1. Tamal was going to bury Prabhupad in lime which decomposes the body immediately to remove any evidence. However, Narayan Maharaj interrupted him and had it done in the authentic manner in salt which all gurus are buried in to keep the body from decomposing and this is a historic custom to be buried in salt. And the fact that Tamal was trying to use lime which goes against the entire historic way of burying gurus, is a proof in itself.

2. When Bhavananda shot two men who were returning to kill him, he said that Jayapataka told him that Prabhupad was very pleased with him for protecting the Deities by shooting these two men. Prabhupad would never have said that by killing 2 men simply to protect the Deities, that's not the way a saintly person thinks. And we know that Sadadanya, also a horrific child molester, was the legal man for Bhavananda who got him off free from any charges and Sadadanya was the one who brought the poison from the CIA agent.

3. Bhavananda used the money that we collected here in Australia to pay for the transgender operation on the

boy he initiated here.

4. Bhavananda is saying on a video "shoot them in the head!" in regards to heroine dealers but he himself was growing opium on our farm in Melbourne for the government which means the CIA.

5. In the Gita, Krishna outlines the demonic qualities which Bhavananda exhibits in full: harshness, arrogance, deceitfulness, pride, etc.

6. Gauridas Pandit was Prabhupad's servant and he was electrocuted in Prabhupad's room and almost died. Bhavananda then became the servant but the question is why would Prabhupad have exposed wires in his own room.

7. Bhavananda was dealing in arms and was the only one in ISKCON with a gun.

8. After Tamal was killed, his body was beaten 42 times with an iron bar by a young boy that Bhavananda had forced to do it. Apparently it was done so that Tamal's body could be put in posture for some Samadhi, but this displays Bhavananda's actual nature because he

had to be in charge with ISKCON and Tamal was the only one in his way. This is proven in the video that I have included in the website with Tamal saying "that firstly 9 men were elected and Jayapataka and Bhavananda's name were not on that list but due to blackmail were added later.

9. One more thing, Bhavananda was also seen coming out of a gay brothel in Thailand while he was still a guru and he started the mardigras in Australia which is a gay celebration in Sydney. I've research what the name Baccus means which is his surname and it is Greek God of intoxication and fornication.

10. I am going to add more detail about this and other aspects on my website in audio to it is easier to listen to but allow me to wrap the book up now as we need to get it published urgently.

11. Jvalamukhi says in her video that Bhavananda was engaging in the satanic ritual child abuse while she was a young girl. She mentions his name in the videos and provided them on my website. She actually goes into trauma when she remembers his name.

12. Bhavananda himself said to Nanda Kumar who was Prabhupad's bodyguard and who decided to leave as he knew the poison was happening, "Don't leave now, we're just slicing up the pie."

13. He also said to Prabhupad's disciples who have mostly left the movement now, "Go ahead and leave, we have our disciples now."

14. He also stood on a picnic chair after blackmailing Tamal to put him on the list of 11 gurus and shouted, "Power, power, power!"

15. The GBC (governing body commission) paid to get a book printed trying to debunk the poisoning, as their positions were all at stake, saying that hair clippers have a cadmium coating and therefore the cadmium poisoning does not hold. However, those samples were taken long before the real poisoning from Adikesava's father was administered, which was only in the last few days.

16. A video has just been released from the daughter of the man I used to sell books with on the street who was raped repeatedly by Bhavananda, sex trafficked in

ISKCON and details the truth that it was all satanic ritual abuse happening in ISKCON.

17. The GBC said that the cadmium was due to the fact that cadmium is used as a coating on hair clippers. And that was the whole argument to dismiss the entire case. However, Nityananda Das had the hair clippers tested and there was no cadmium on them. So as I thought the GBC made that story up, cadmium is not used on hair clippers.

18. The devotee I started selling books with was ordered by Bhavananda to kill the devotee in Australia who was exposing him. He had to arrange a team to bury the body on a new Govaidhan farm. He was then ordered to kill another devotee and that's when he refuses and this devotee was engaged in all black magic rituals with Bhavananda.

19. There is a girl in Melbourne, Polly Woodward, who is the daughter of the man I started selling books with, Jagadatma who has come forward since I started this book. She is saying that she was repeatedly raped by Bhavananda and that her father was told by

Bhavananda to kill three devotees who knew about Bhavananda's activities. And on the third person he refused. All the details will be included on the website. As well as she was photographed naked with Gour Govinda swami, who had been drugged in order to get the photo.

20. Prabhupad asked Srila Govinda to take care of his ISKCON, and this would be the reason why Bhavananda send a bomb to blow up their Ashram.

Bhavananda pretended to do Caturmasya, which entails eating off the ground gruel once a day.

However he cheated and was importing alcohol and adrenochrome and all sorts of foods into his room.

However, the three months would have built up his animosity and hate toward Prabhupad, that although he was doing it for fame, the inconvenience would have turned to a deadly rage.